GORGEOUS PLUNGE

MICHAEL GOTTLIEB

ROOF BOOKS
NEW YORK

for
Alan Davies

Grateful acknowledgment to the editors of the following publications in which some of this work originally appeared: *Angle, First Intensity, Kenning, Lingo, Philly Talks, Poetics Journal, PotePoetzine, Ribot, Snare, Torque.* "The Night Book" originally appeared as a chapbook published by Other Publications in 1998.

Cover and illustrations ©1999 Mark Saltz.
Author photograph ©1999 Peter Halle.

Roof Books are distributed by Small Press Distribution,
1341 Seventh Avenue, Berkeley, CA. 94710-1403.
Phone orders: 800-869-7553

 State of the Arts This book was made possible, in part, by a grant from the New York State Council on the Arts.

NYSCA

ROOF BOOKS
are published by Segue Foundation
303 East 8th Street
New York, NY 10009

GORGEOUS PLUNGE

CONTENTS

The Night Book

for Alvin Feinman and Michael Gizzi

"Bring out your dead."

♦

Cloud cuckooland
---*if only.*

A kind of wishful preposterism...

Sinkingly,
like your dawn's daily drowning
in the workaday light,

there it is again,
that tang,

that lusty, unfeeling
plashing of pellucidity.

Tremens, spots, a certain sagging,
that shadow on the film

---we'd just love to write them off.

But these too
I fear
are too true.

♦

What youthful offenders
we once fancied ourselves.

The consolations of
incorrigibility...

as if there were heroics in that.

You want to say,
"I did what I did
so you wouldn't have to."

Unproven kidney.

The lonely gunmen, us, cavorting.

♦

Guilty knowledge

as if there could be any other.

Like being grandfathered in,
no one else wants to remember
so it falls to you.

But who knew, then?

Hiving off.

Cadences of the
seemingly uneducable.

Covering for our fallen comrades.

♦

Pace the sage
of Washington Square Village:

"It is good to be the poet,
until you're thirty-five..."

Whipsawed knee plays.

As one learns
that zero
is not a vowel.

Wasting and etiolation,
those novel mediums.

Despondency rates.

A self collar.
For each of us,
a personal oblast.

"...just make it to your sixties,

that's the trick."

♦

For the

foregone

gone.

11

◆

A guide to the lower slopes
of infamy...

The faint praise
read in the weak smile.

While, back in
their superior normality,

cruising the pejorative,
here come the insincere corrections:
"I never thought of that."

When they say,
"I'm sure you know
what you're doing."

"We look forward with interest
to observing your progress."

The full-daughter spectrum
of casuistry.

◆

That grand fallacy
we cannot help but entertain
---this is just
 some sort of jest.

What you don't want
to see,

laid out as panoply.

This pathology of hope.

"How do you not look upon
what your eyes show you
when you close them?"

To the extent that every drama
is a serial
of squandered opportunity.

◆

And who are these,

in their masks and gowns;
their parti-colored head coverings
like so many carefree berets?

A sort of
Bohemian Coast Guard
I think,
essaying a rescue
against some forlorn shore.

Drawn up against the lee,
a knot of miserable survivors,
among them the Duke,
his malevolent major domo,
and his long-lost sister,
traveling incognito
disguised as a servant-boy;

all huddled up together,

caught in the searching glare
of the surgical theatre.

♦

The not-so-young dead

we're not quite old enough
to mourn properly.

♦

The grosgrain of our day
where we stipple and elide,
navigating the round.

Pallid tin of the original:
when I look at yours,
then look back at mine.

That I am still lying here
yet another night

must diminish me
further.

♦

Offhandedly,
your keeper spared me a minute...

"Show me the talking cure
and I'll show you
the talking horse."

Sketching with her fingers a net,
an image rent:

just so,
that's how far gone you were.

♦

The shapeless within us.

"I wouldn't want
to be bothered with me either."

Heaped,
so much firewood.

What we shrink from.

These orphaned,
perambulating,
countersunk syncopations,
from abstention
to denial.

These conversations with those
we will never lay eyes on again,

or have as little chance of meeting
as...

And those epic, wasted, colloquies

15

with those who rule
our internal lies.

♦

The anomic findings.

"I think you'd better look at this."

The exaggerated restraint.

"I'd like to say
I never think about it
anymore."

Briefing.
Deploying.
Saddling the mounts.
They who style themselves
as mendicants.

The ones
who hunt together.

♦

We make as to gauge
the irresistible seeping.

A kind of foetor of longing.

Like a claim
upon our rents.

16

Throwing us back
upon our losses.

This seething flight,
every aging minute.

♦

You want to say,
"Yes, I was looking forward
to this abyss."

Always believing
this was the just reward.

You realize then
no one ever puts it quite that way.

For good reason.

♦

The problem
is not with the emotion,
or the recollecting.

It's the tranquillity.

♦

A finger writing on the grime.

Wash me.

Pass,
don't pass.

Left for dead,
right for alive.

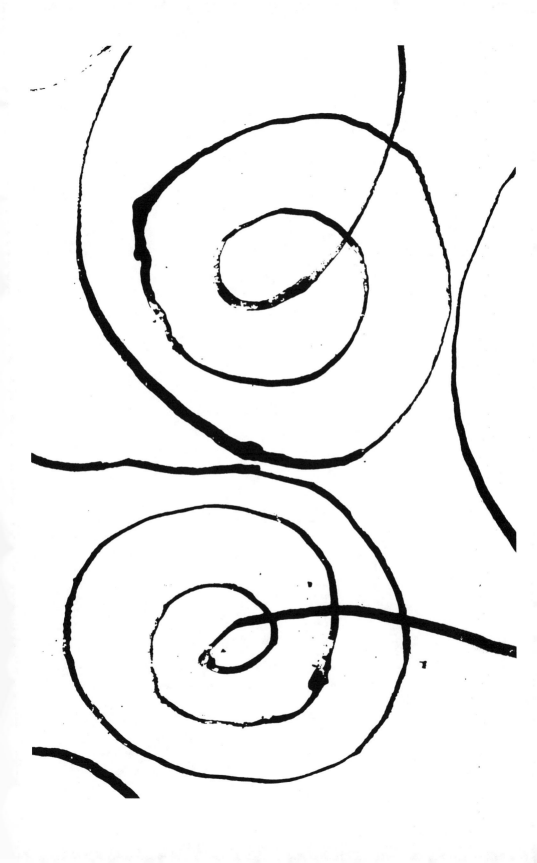

Gorgeous Plunge

1. What Doesn't Kill Us Makes Us Weaker

What doesn't kill us makes us weaker.

Across the sky,
a missing man formation.

Like that untoward ardor
for precedence,
that way of styling one's self,
those illiberal disaffections,
all speaking so poorly
for our powers of abeyance, inference,
investiture, endurance.

In this lattice of derision,

a ragtag, a nattered remainder,
calumnied, unweighted.
They are waiting here,
the company entire.

That is not really us,
we say,
"Just because it's in my car,
doesn't mean it's mine."

The unnumbered lot.

The waste plot.

The stringently incurious
applying the barmecide,
administering the drubbing anew.

The whirling disease.

Not enough,
never nearly enough
of---

the merry men,

the past masters,

---they were here just a minute ago.

This can kill you too,
just as easily:
too much poetry.

Poetry can be bad for your health.

The ones dragged along,
driven off,
ridden to exhaustion, to distraction,
to all ends,
driven down.

Withering under
the pitying exposure.

Do not shake.

The appalling results.

The old fashioneds, the manhattans,
the last of the delawares.
The trophies and the captives---
here on the Northern Branch,
along with the fragiles
and the rushes and the ground rates.

Raised, that is organized,
fully subscribed, like a hopeful, fated regiment,
at first sight,
upon first publication.

Point away from face
and other people
while opening.

We become our lists.

2. Cast Into The Outer Part

Cast into the outer part
of your darkness
again.

I want to ask,

this---it was *this*, wasn't it---
we wanted to think
there could be nothing finer
than to be condemned
to do this all day,
but it is *this* thing, is it not,
that is killing you---

You, who have more time for this
than any of us.

That giddy egg-shell titter
we hear it even here,

this silted-up aisle,
this foxed corner,
this tenebrous rec room.

Look at us.

Decline. Demise.
Shopping for a full stop.

There are bad actors
and there are cloaking forces.
There are disarming agents.

Look upon them.
Look upon their works:

the fade, the descenders,
the diminishing plangent.

When it doesn't like
what it hears

it shuts us up.

The tear aways.
The straining dollies,
the overreaching, countervailing error,
the wet signature,
the shadow of the proseator.

There is a malign muse.

3. The People Have Not Spoken

The people have not spoken.

They have nothing to say.

Or, perhaps, they're too busy
to get back to us.

Likewise, by now
we must be alive to the suggestion
that he is in fact dead

or should be, by all rights.

The one time
he was one with the world
was when he was doing the one thing
the world could have cared less about.

"It's what makes us
no good for anything else."

Chance has nothing whatsoever to do with it,
with these sallow, coruscating, sheepishly bilious delectations.

The fun house mirror.
The guttering lamp.

"Here's looking like you."

A wail of obeisance
rising from the dark.
We hear it in the swelling.

The problem with only liking
that, and those
who like you back.

Brutishness, for example,
as a beard for
something far worse.

The inattentive thief, the saintly actuary,
the altruistic scavenger,
the vexed, the ulcerative,
the shadow dominion.

This is what waits for us.

"If you keep scratching it
it will bleed."

This is the grove, this is the glade
this is the place
where they took the best part of us away.

In the same way that
for every buyer
there must a seller be,

you cannot rise
without my falling.

And so, when you go to sleep
you will see me
holding your hand.

4. *"Death Or The Booby Hatch"*

"Death or the booby hatch,"
---that is the choice, according to Nick.

The victims of this knowledge,
with their unsecuritized affirmations,

their skin, itself a kind of outerwear
shrunk, lines pulled like a wrapper,
scarred with declined verbs,
the kind
we don't care to admit escape from our lips.

This is what that life provides you,
those teeth in the head,
that cough,
if you're lucky.

This great predicate
giving way to
a sublunary subjunctive.

This pondering weight,
a plumage
in service of this familiar horror,
rising hereabouts,
...it's not that there are none as bad,
it's just that
there are so many of them.

Then there are
the other ones, who rise.

Our portion control,

our job,
to abandon all hope.

True humility,
the most uncompromising
in the arsenal.

We do not rise
to that occasion.

As if making it new
makes us old,
and so in the end
kills us.

We die
so others can be free

to ignore us.

5. *Having Said That*

Having said that.

The vindicated.

The arrested pose
in the face of
the wayward tally.

The cautionary hives,
the indifferent begging,
the great calumniator
encountering, at speed,
the downgraded, the unalloyed,
the spill of dismay.

"I took out all those loans,
for this?"

"I would hate to trouble you,
but I would have no trouble
hating you."

"No one sleeps in this hotel,
sonny."

That's another whole tranche
we can do without.
Think of them as
ungermane small holders.

The unredoubtable,
the easy virtue,
the meager verification.

The appellant inconsistencies.

The sick-making realization.

A set-to in the alcove.

"I can't compete
with *that*."

Taking its course,
the eery derision;
the poet's poet,
unsteady on his, or her, pins,
counting to ten,
or is it five?
Muttering all the while,
"This does not scan."

One week a year, maybe two
you wear the funny hat,
you drink the funny drink,
you shake the secret handshake.

As if we're doing our national service,
the other fifty weeks we're reservists;
our employers are supposed to let us go
and not hold it against us.

Like a kind of jury duty
we keep getting called to.

But we never seem to vote
on a verdict.

We keep getting hung.

And every year

we're called back for more.

Here it is again,
that slip in the mail.

There's some Norman O. Goodman,
a clerk of this court,
who just won't let go.

6. The Extremes

The extremes.

Going there.

While
we are all trapped,
only a few of us
chew off our hindquarters.

Listing, taking on water,
in this vessel,
this poor, freakish raft.

That progressive chord
we cannot help but hear
as a deflated assent.

There must have been
many amongst us
who you would have expected
to misplace by now.

Suffering from a cunning.

Helpless in the eddies,
no matter how we struggle,
while, to the casual observer---

It is as if our anger
and our fear
keep us as young
as we remain.

A smiling defiance,

at least that's how we try and sell it.

A kind of *apnea aforethought.*

A wishful drag
on the free flow of
the falling.

And is there no relationship
between what happens to you
and what you happen to do?

A case of gross exceptionalism.
A revolting ascendancy.
The monotone behind the tocsin.

If it was only a case
of simply outshouting,
then, a page a week
would seem like a lot to me.

As if the moment we let up,
if it wasn't for this grippe,
we'd be gone too.

The fallen
among us.

Maybe this is what recovery, regaining health,
is all about,
it just feels like its opposite.

Surely, it is not as if
you had never gotten better before.

7. The Sustained Siege

The sustained siege.

The great teeth and
the mighty jaws.

Pretending
that these tails are not lashing,
that these blows
are not coming fast and low,
that these are not
our vitals, so stapped.

Like a fervid gift
for deflection.

"If it's not yours
perforce
it's mine,
even if I never use it."

"I can't carry you anymore,
you don't weigh enough."

Orphaned all,

a descending series
we are obliged to appraise,
like a kind of metrical test,

the dreadfully unkeyed
mirrored phrasings,
the anguished, somnolent draughts
streaming back empty,

the smoking cliffs,
the empty loges,
the halls where the insults
were first tossed.

All of us entirely under-rehearsed.

The atrophied, antic, strophes.

The arbitrarily endurable,
the purblind tolling,
the graven, wan,
detuned verging.

These gravid,
"posthumously born."

The giving up
---that makes it official.

The suspicious rising
and the cheered fall.

The stingy padding,
the lack of anything we would recognize
as insulation.

Jinking left and right,
availing not.

"I can't shake them."

Sunk to the axles.

"This time
it's not different."

8. A Robust Little Microbe

A robust little microbe
descends to our level.

As if there was nothing worth
mentioning in between:
on the one hand the podium finish,
on the other, internal exile.

Poetry as
giving comfort to your enemies.

Duped, then deduped.

The immodest glee in the cell.
The denatured tolling.
The Great Unwell.

Over here,
the martyr of the Via Po,
embracing a cart horse.
The beast,
fallen in its traces,
pawing the mud.
Never to rise again.

The question that is begged.

What happens
when we have nothing
left to feed it?

It's not estrangement,
it's not like he needs some 'strange.'

Twenty or thirty years later
it's become part of his
unique selling proposition,
his customized defeat.

They say it is an allowance,
we don't have to pay it back
right away,

it's kind of like carrying water
for them,
it's alright for awhile,
if you don't get thirsty.

When they said "crush" for the first time,
as in, "he needs to be crushed,"
we assumed it was for the benefit
of different audience.

A double line
to put underneath
all that had been said earlier.

As if
it was only a little
freshet of ire.

9. An Expulsion Order

An expulsion order.

A vaulting sob.

The truckling, the grim connivance,
the makeshift suffrage, the crown of the road,
the foisted coincidences,
the vans with no windows,
the special clips and rosettes.

What was,
what never was.

Those exculpations, they always seemed slurred,
we watched them fly forth
utterly without any assistance on our part,
as we, equally unbidden, find ourselves
proffering excuses:

"If two is the recommended dosage,
then five must be so much better,
that much more effective.
It only follows."

Because they knew exactly
what was going into the sauce,
as it were,
and had every opportunity,
to stand-to with aid
---that made it all the worse;

and later,
we came to recognize

that as a trait of the control group.

The eyries of the craven,

always picked so clean,
the dirt weighs so much less that far up.

Suffering us to approach,
we are charmed, delighted
by how much he really knows,
about us---of all people.
How did he learn all this stuff?

A couple of disarmingly tuned references
and he's off.

"First we have to decide
which garbage belongs to you.
Then, do you get any water rights?"

The violacious predations.
The swarming odds,
the treeless blunders,
the stunner, a prefigured
quiddity that fits us all.

You couldn't have known.
There were too many of them.

It's as hard as getting promoted
in a peacetime army.

That's why we needed this,
think of it as a tidy little war.

All the ones
we forgot we knew:

he's gone.
Him too.
All of them.

Like we're stuck here,
and this is some sort of garrison town.

He bounces, he veers,
he careers about the ville.

Someone keeps winding him up.

10. *Those Happy Few Years*

Those happy few years.

Among all the youths---

you alone are left
to tell the tale.

At the time,
nothing but unproved deposits.

Exploratory wells.

Was there ever enough there
for all of us?

Then, almost before we knew it,
resettled in these oddly empty villages.

It's not work that we're used to.

What work would be?

A kind of Travelers Aid.

A monstrous pageant
of fleeing suspects.

Here, the overgrown cuts,
the telephone poles,
the tooth picks and dead hangers
of a typical secondary market
conspiring now to shut out the light
that we are convinced

we were promised.

Instead
formed up in a hollow square
at the designated place.

And how had *he*,

of all of us, the most careless,
apparently the least
inclined for this
terrible life,

how had he remained at large
so long?

Brushing up against it,
the full-blown,
the leafing out.

It's like a condition,

but we keep at it, for "love of the craft,"
because "we think this is important."

So here we are,
year after year,
repeating---

"I just live for *this*."

A strange sinking of heart,
the weight of something hardening,
the way it inexplicably swamps some,
while others it buoys up,
as they bob off into their future.

The swelling always goes down
eventually.

*Don't envy yourself
just yet.*

Wicking us,
soul by soul,
back into the dark warp.

If it wasn't for poetry
we could have been happy,
we would have been satisfied,
content with our lot.

And when it came to our lot,
of one thing I am sure:
there would have been a lot more of it.

11. Here Is The Painted Steel

Here is the painted steel.

And here is where someone
has repeatedly brushed over the rust.

The airport art,
the broad daylight,
the impassive patron,
the space heater,
the convert that remains,
the brave fire,
the obtaining leeds,
the predated checks,
the pretersensuous carrier,
the seam that is not taped,
the finish that is giving something away,
the wear marks,
the run of the town,
the walk up wake up.

Because it's Corten
it is supposed to rust.

This is what used to be called
the high life.

Messing along at this elevation.

A kind of
self dosage.

That's what these ropes are here for,
to keep you on your toes.

This will be accounted among you
as a respectable haul.

As we all learn
there is no drama without concealment.

Back in Bolton Landing,
before heading out of an evening,
he loads the plates
in the bed of the pick up,
just so.

We give our parole.
We have to.

We have to be
our own worst enemies.

It isn't important for any of these reasons.
It's not important because you say it is.

It is important because
you cannot say it at all.

It was as if all this,
all these riches,
were denominated
in some completely unconvertible currency.

Look how much it weighs.
What do you do with it all?

This is how the news is discounted by the traders.

Increasingly distracted.
Always, that quietism.

Like the abandonment of a district.

What you decide
you must to learn to swallow,
like asking,

"Would they have ended up
like this anyway?"

Like knowing,
for sure.

12. The Wreck Of The Happenstance

The wreck of the happenstance:

you can't have it your way,
you can't have it both ways,
you can't have it.

Between what we should have
and what we must,

where the fray-dust rises.

We scrub for the chance operation.
You never know.

There are always too many
middle aged poets
to go around.

"Survival can be such a bother."

A kind of at-home demonstration:
I am here to show you
what not to do.

What we call stabilizing the ruins.

This is the death dealing one.
A kind of Munchausen's schadenfreude,
by default.

Where the shadows play
and the graphomania becomes pronounced,

where the 'about' comes around.

It's always interesting
to see who loses it at the first turn,
who drops out in the middle goings,
which ones look like they are going to go all the way
and blow up right before the end.

It's about pacing yourself.
The maintenance schedule.
The manufacturer's recommendation.

On the other hand,
there's so much to be said
for that blooming fall,
the progressive unfurling,
the awful flame.

The comprehension of how something is built
that can only come from cleaning it,
or taking it apart,
or smashing it.

13. *Something Terrible Always Happens*

Something terrible always happens
in the end.

A kind of cladding,
the sort that is intended to
show the progress of the intrusion,
to get it to expend its force
at the distant reaches of the concern.

The frontier
and the back tier.

We'll put a wall there,
and invest it
with a troop of justifications.

The moral agency
we bring to this *want.*

There is a tyranny
among the exponents.

The celestial navigation taught on Utopia Parkway.

And sleeping over here---
Queen,
King,
California King.

That particular uncharacteristically
blowzy turn of phrase
we came to associate with him,
the way he used to mock his own piety;

the blond and the gray,
and the scalp.

"A shade of my former self."

"Just like me, but better."

All those years,
one long struggle session.

The intact
and the sundered.

We live it out loud,
in the company of our friends,
and everyone else.

It's no use
watching your words,
they're not yours anymore.

The brutal, dilatory call-backs,
the limited sight distance,
the insincere ink,
the nasty little unchecked baggage,
the inartful remodeling,
what we dine out on,
what we leave out in the rain,
what we hope the coping
will deal with,
the sorry betterment,

the brief flashes of what we
remember him for.

This terra damnata
where smoke falls

wreathed in grimaces

and everything we thought we'd buried
keeps returning
for another rending look-see.

It's a kind of mentation,
a disordered back-formation
we found here,
under the bland assurance...

Everything is not alright.
It never was.
It never will be.

14. The Way He Presents

The way he presents,
this is his address,
this trackless jilting,
this rapid descent,
this scabbing-over,
this disinclination to discuss
our less successful efforts at pleonasm,
our new outcomes policy,
the way we crack and peel,
the beauty part,
falling down gently.

This is no distraction,
this is what is it all about,
why we are here today,
on these serried couches.

The debased orders,
sitting over there
with something lingering
of their former hauteur
in the ragged assumptions,
the scattered defiance,
the enfeebled entablature.

This is the end-stage.

The night soil of all our ambitions.

Something is approaching
at a dead run.

Here, in the chuff

of my palm,
you can feel it too,
right now
it's still small.
It's just starting out.

You can limn this
as easy as me.
These are the massed bands,
these are the dress bluffs,
these are the absolute modifiers,
these are the once imposing gates
and here are the neglected grounds.

This was once a tended argument,
well drained, company water,
good gravel bottom,
with commanding views
of the receding replies.

15. I See You Still
On The Corner Of Lafayette

I see you still on the corner of Lafayette,
in front of Puck himself,
kissing us all on the lips
before making your way back to Brooklyn.

In this
eldritch darkness
I can hear your breath,
I can see the outlines
of your reply.

A water feature,
that's all this is...
a minor hazard, a kind of jest.

The nascence of the order.

The causal disregard.

The pennants fixed to the whip antennas.

Standing in the turret,
oblivious to the falling shells,
directing fire with a smile playing along his features,
bareheaded.

"I don't know where it comes from."

The innards,
the coils of the claims,
the parts we're not meant to see.

"This enough for you?"

In the sorry lobby
History, a surly, roused night clerk
shuffles to the counter
and negligently flips open the ledger.

That dispassionate coherence
the world has come to expect of us.

The sheer disablement.

What we have come to tolerate.

It is a settlement,
like putting our English into receivership,
mouthing the lines about gentle persevering
that we've all been taught to pass on.

There are, it is averred, laws for poets too.

We search out the pinched looks,
the all-too-innocent,
the overly generous.

We tease out,
we lose count,
we avert our eyes,
we recall the ingenuity
we always intended.

The thick air
quite nearly holds us up.

Over here, the singing nettles.

Poetry may not be a revealed religion.

There are bad days and there are worse.

Here for awhile.

Now gone.

In that
gorgeous plunge.

The Staging Areas

Take Gloversville.

As good a point as any to start from.

It's not like they made millinery there.

♦

There,
in the Ninety-Third Minute,

the tentative palings,
like the underpainted palisades
across the river,

all the accustomed asperity
that had accompanied us thus far,
all in a moment,

like the vanishing point,

utterly gone.

♦

The master of perspective,
drawn up
in front of the tooth glass
reviews his posish...

He is not dissatisfied.

"*Perishables.*
That a good name for them,"
he muses.

While the afternoon before the party
the big man on the hippocampus asks,

"what happens
when we run out of people
we've decided not to talk to?"

But by then it's too late.

♦

It's not like
we're trying to avoid the subject,
but here, on the Great Ring Road

we really get to cover a lot of ground
without ever having to go downtown.

Of course,
there's always
the not entirely unreasonable fear

that all this inarguable predication
of discerning principle

will one day, and one day soon
be revealed as nothing more

than a somewhat unimproved
detour.

♦

The spring-loaded implements.

That unique, gravity-fed discipline.

The purposely untended countertop.

The entire enterprise---
a scheme too diabolical
to recount in mixed company.

With a mocking air of personalization about it,
like something with a *Swank* label on it.

Posting
to a punishment battalion.

Transportation,
in the older sense.

Freighted with chains
of our own forging.

Looming from the dark,

some sort of punitive rest stop.

♦

What we most decidedly
don't want to hear.

A kind of demand note.

A demarche.

"Well and truly bent,"
comes the voice from under the hood.

Though the mass of it is not,
as it turns out,
shrunken at all.

"I just thought you'd want to be aware."

In that piquant way that advice itself
so often transmutes into a sort of aggression.

"If I didn't pay for it
I'm not afraid of it."

♦

Bearing it in mind.

As if it is something you carry.

Bearing it before you.

You too:
a bearer, in train.

The approaches.
The marches.
The first camps.

Like citations,
agate notices,
decorations from defunct instrumentalities.
"I too was there."

♦

Those endless, wintered-over aforethoughts.

More false dawns
treading the unchartered streets.

What, finally, we get known for.

Guarding your squares
and your magazines.

How you come to resemble them.

The hastily thrown up defenses
by the terminus.

Your voice on the steps outside.

If not for that irresolute moment
upon the barricade,
today we might all be speaking English.

Your animadversions.

"You
slay
me."

◆

The siding
where we are left to lay up.

The all too eagerly awaited tea trolley.

The faintest sketch.

Plucking the strings now
from a creaking lyre-back chair.

This last, worst place,
where you can't be ambiguous,
even to yourself.

♦

A legend that has been stamped on our papers.

Notwithstanding
the pier glass that tells nothing:

there *are* secret cities here.

Closed provinces.

All of us carrying internal cartes de visite,
the kind we drop upon ourselves.

What you or I would consider an acceptable loss,

the sort of thing the windshield claims,

becomes, for our friend here,
a bellwether of special pleading...

"I claim this land for spleen."

And so are we inscribed, one and all.

♦

A lot of knowledge
is a dangerous thing,
I think.

The calamitous momentum.

The foreboding repose.

Sentencing, rendering, dunning.

Like that apparently irrational desire
to go to sleep in the snow.

Not again.
Once more.
As well as.

"How often
it is what you do know
that can hurt you."

♦

So,
to the gods of increase
we aver,
"it's not mine,
I never saw it before."

People grow this in their backyards
up and down the East Coast:

it's *shame*,

welling up eternal,
busy at its trade.

The crews working at the levers
of appearance.

Action along the surfaces.

Mining the roundhouses and the trestles.

The object of all that opprobrium,
spirited out of the salon.

The inevitable crush at the platform.

An ignominious disguise.

A kind of mimicry of our
fecklessnesses.

♦

The chain mail.

The channel packet.

The perfect binding.

The structured query.

The loose strife.

"---What else do I have to show for this?"

The flying squad.

The winged shuttle.

The sorely flashing.

The sharply flung.

The fleeing.

♦

The brown fields
over there,
by the banks of the burning shore.

It's not as if
we're soiling ourselves
with this knowledge.

None of us in terrifically good odor.

The cracked plaques, the reliefs underfoot.

"Wouldn't we remember
if we hadn't been here
at least once before?"

♦

A not unpenetrating approbation,
along the lines of,
"I should have killed you when I had the chance."

Or,
"In this way, my friend,
all exuberance is irrational."

"...It's one of the Four Freedoms,
the one no one ever talks about."

And none of us
can remember a different time.
Though it's not because
we're not old enough.

♦

The price look up.

The date time stamp.

The call tags.

The score keeping units.

The sizing in the material.

The fruits of the search.

The calmly recalcitrant shallows.

The door prize.

The unquick.

The revolving blast door.

The proxy whinging.

The humbling gag reflex.

The sheering.

A blue that becomes black.

The hideous symptoms.

The meteorological feature.

A collusion of indicators.

The unnatural bar.

A pacific gigantism.

"Above us
only
sky."

♦

What we were allowed to play with,
what we were slated for,
before the first culling.

This is where we used to sit,
and call out the iterations of the clouds,
white and rose and white,
as they assembled themselves for us,

sallying forth from their airy ports

---just the sort of thing,
we assured ourselves back then,
we would certainly never be able to summon up
in even a few years' time, much less a decade or two---

as the massive dreams descanted across our skies,

every of them replete, entire,
realized with that flush, heartless, dazzling articulation.

And so, of course, we were wrong.

We were not fortunate enough
to forget any of this.

A caution and a despite,

a reminder of what we've settled for.

They abide, forever fixed,
for us, in us,
soaring there still
through that ancient azure afternoon.

◆

The wildly depatterned
not unaffecting contrast.

Losing them in the lights.

The higher order functions
sailing under a flag of convenience.

Making for the anchorage.

The uncontrite arbiters
gathering a head of steam.

The carrying voice
and what it cedes.

The manipulated signals.

The determined little fellow
in his sealed train.

◆

Distributing the spoilage.

Amiable impunity.

Aggravated assault, of sorts.

The blackguards walking backwards,
not really retreating;

instead, casting aspersions
in the opposite direction.

"Here they come again."

That somewhat dashed expression,
lost in the thriving crowd,

as the cruel tidings sink in:

we all have to make representations,

we all need to table certain notions.

♦

Pathos by the running foot.

And then
that inconstant, darkling breeze

and the snatched phrase it carried,
eventually bringing us in among

the sore, fagged outliers,
the ones that hadn't yet fled,
humming, or were they moaning,
before their tumble-down huts.

If I didn't know better
I'd have to say
they seem oddly familiar,

the struck-off, cashiered,
consummately impugned,

even now
sitting this afternoon here beside us,

these few remaining,
as good as lost, unlamented
hell dwellers.

What is there left to say to them?

Yes, I have no excuses.
I have no excuses today.

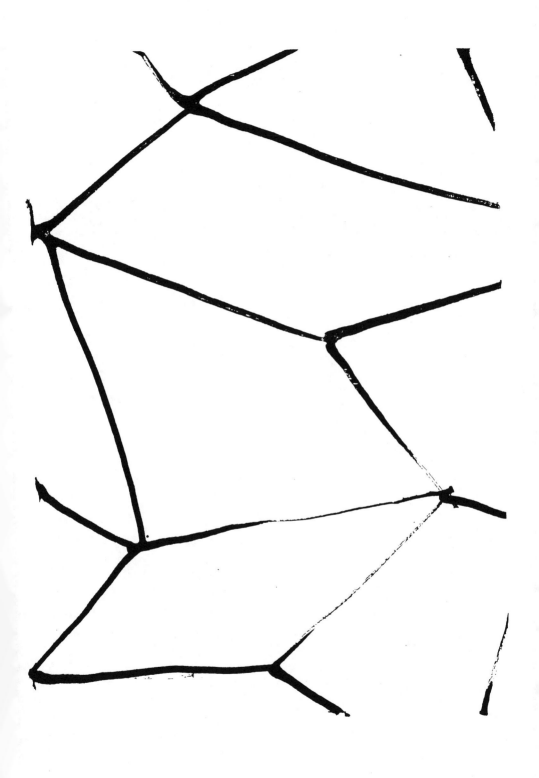

The Sick Man Of Kenmare Street

Becalmed.
No calm.

The Sick Man of Kenmare Street
again finds himself
confounded by rebellion.

As if there are any causes
that are natural.

A mouthful of *offends*...

Any less would be
all too human.

Like so many mere shakings.

After all else,
everyone,
everything that could adhere,
has absconded.

Even the ill-fitting,
jumped-up embarrassments.

The swiftly superannuated.

Half lost in a flare of inanition.

All that is left at the bottom
of the bag.

Impaired Impulse Control

As easy as,
"kiss your hand."

Another example of
impaired impulse control.

Not a sabbatical,
a leave.

I knew if I forgot you would remind me.

Where the landing once led,
overgrown garden apartments,
the edge of a downs,
a degrading trail of cinder.

Like the hapless crew
hoping for a shop steward.

Hypnotic collusion.

The kind of inexplicable enrichment
that once was a crime
in these parts.

"As if
we deserved better."

Like An Aryan From Darien

Agape,
like an Aryan from Darien
tottering before a stair
of disused expectations.

What we thought,
where we could,
when it was still just us.
And we mattered.

"But the histrionics were always
on their side."

A cuff across the face,
fashioned from neglect
and ague.

Disowned tools.

We couldn't really say
we were receiving
the time value of our money.

A gross insult.

Not just a little refractory.

The proximate cause.

Your canceled check is your receipt.

The Be-All And End-All
Of Mr. Amdahl

Lifting bodies.

Cast-off quota blocks,
massive, converging.

Methodological excesses,
not to mention
symbol mongering.

Another well regarded fool
earns his
protective coloration.

Sort of like a geode:
cracking open with a mere tap
---the interior
a wondrous gem of revelation.
But what do you do with him then?

The be-all and end-all of Mr. Amdahl.
"I'll meet you down by the mood swings."

"Myoclonic jerks
---that's us!"

That Totalizing, Abjectly Benign Dressing Of Bonhomie

A disquieted watermark.

If only they had smaller pieces of paper
we wouldn't be stuck with so many epigrams.

Deposed calamities.

Right here,
under the present circumstances,
drizzled with that totalizing, abjectly benign
dressing of bonhomie,
there lies
a milling colony
of voracious regret.

The numinous spawn
of our progenitive argument:

rimless dejections,
stoved-in compromise,
batteries of justification.

Begrudging culls.

The Loss Leader

The belying regard,
the garnisheed inflections,
the berating remittance,
the induced protestation,
the belittling reprise.

A noisome regalia.

An avocation for *practice*.
means
short work with the likes of them.

The memory,
a quizzical armature,
what was left of it,
showered with darkness.

"As if we care" ---a pennant
streaming from the yawning heights.

Travelers in the region
report wholesale abandonment.

The consummation of long exposure:
gone to pieces.

The is
the loss leader.

The Vapors

The berserk:
As if there could be any doubt,
here's the place
they start from
when they go there.

The vapors among us,
motile,
sibilant.

A grievance
foundering in mortality.

Where the seams
finally part,
and all that was bearable
seeps away
to a vast, unregarding
admittance.

"You can't just
toss it in your pocket
and traipse around
like that."

Expended salutations.

Prostrate banter.

Over here,
the bright untrodden field.

Harvesting Disclaimers

Up there,
at ten o'clock,
there's something
I don't like the looks of.

A front rolling into town,
harvesting disclaimers.

Calling attributes.

Remote ballast.

*You will step on the soil
of many countries.*

*Your dearest wish
will come true.*

The hegemon
over the horizon,
fumbling through his missal.

The Entelechy Society
at azimuth.

The dying fall.

"Now hear this."

Off You Go

Another heedless vessel
softly, against the disprized bumpers,
offering his lays,

arranging his instrumentalities.

The sharps should be deposited in the indicated slot.

The root of all our trouble:
"too many tall pea pods?"

Revisiting the modus vivendum,
the soaring languishing,
enforced, like a kind of oral hygiene.

"If I had as much time
as you
for this sort of thing,
my resume would be as long
as yours."

So,
off you go.

Wholesale Predictors

The brays, the graceless motes.

Deaccessioning the wits.

I had it here a moment ago, I'm sure I did.

The sentiment from the provinces,.
unrecognized, disordered.

A minute fugitive proceeding.

In this chamber, the once sunny mass noun
fallen upon less credulous times.

And even in the window treatments
there is that reek.

Anticipating the heavily policed potlatch
we know we have coming to us;
here we are in the meantime,
dowsing for superlatives.

Waiting on.
whiling away,
casting about for
the ritual debasement.

The terms and conditions
of that derangement of the features.

Acidulated,
again and again,
like too much salt in the coffee.

A bereft surfeit.

A Universal Reactor

The ill purposes.
Schools of them.

The sergeant maintains that
greater men than us
have drowned in these whorls.

So easily traduced.
Almost asking for it.

It was much like this,
in a similarly subtle realm,
that we found this place:

a sort of platform of sham attachment,

a kind of depository,
a place of general intake for our accident prone inten-
tions,

it was there that we were dealt
that shrewd wallop.

And so here we are, expelled, out the other end,
the not unscarified remainder: us
---enjoying the peculiarly clarifying perfume
of that last heresy:
indifferentism.

The Silent Treatment

Here it comes again:
that thrumming adumbration.

A corral,
a motley pound,
an afflicted pen,
off on a spare pitch or fill.

A place of summary condemnation.

Pretending that we don't all face it,
the fulminant element.

Of course, we know better;
this isn't really our lot.

It's just a transitive case.

Fending off the prevailing.

The proffered cup.

A Subsyndromal Consanguinity

This is where our ways part.

This is what
it has come to.

Here's a new tempo,
we'll name it argumento.

"I want to go the way she went."

That seamily edenic afternoon
with the shades
drawn.

Like cocktail shakers
beaded with something that was not dew.

Pretending not to notice
the rents in the screening.

It settles provisionally,
like the hesitant solstice-dusk,
upon our shoulders.

As if finally
it was time
to burn the title.

As in,
"I'll take the low road."

The Entry Level Eclogue

This rake, I'm afraid,
has no teeth left.

Unattended exchanges:
this is what our commerce has been reduced to.

"I wanted to tell you how much we missed you."

What was once called a companionway.

Over there,
the abject laity.

It awed us so,
all that audacious debris,
haunting us, cloaking our dismay.

And, in the next heat
the semi-eliminators
will face off.

The Idiocy Of West Village Life

Again we find ourselves
looking for
that very special
data hygiene specialist.

A proleptic mind.
A rogue imagination.
A consummate indoorsman.

Not dissident, diffident...
The difference between
self-effacing
and self-abnegating.

She is simply unbiddable.

Like more emergency eyewash.

This one too is
'good to go.'

New Model Army Resting In The Parks

He hasn't taken leave of his senses.
Just a long weekend.

The uneasy aplomb.

As we too grow inured,
the tell-tale enervation.

A disembodied shellac.
A remarkably resonant hardening.
A long-lived distress.
An impassively obsolescent patent process,
like vulcanization.

"I still find it all very upsetting."

Were we not all once great advocates
of Fair Use doctrine?

The horrid inevitability.

Bantering With The Mangle

The party hat.

The familiar.

The imp.

It's always what we cannot remember
that changes us forever.

A fastness
that was not there yesterday.

A mass, a chaff
of aluminum up there.

Presents of mind.

"They call this new?
Twenty years ago
we were already bored with this."

The always,
the sometimes,
the never.

By all accounts.

The Man-Shaped Shadow

My opposite number,
lopping limbs
as he nears.

New.
Like new.
Almost new.
Better than new.

In the lost precinct of the poets:
wildlife management.

A skill set,
a fabric family,
a title case.

The ingredients, most of them
available at any hardware store.

As the doors slide into their pockets,
an excited utterance:

"I don't know what I like
but I know I don't like you."

A sampler
for disaster.

The Triumph Of Essentialism

Apprehended
fleeing the scene.

The parlous pass
where we find ourselves.

This ejecta:
what's left after the service life,
the duty cycle;
like the stranded costs
you can never recover.

A run of dismaying chicanes.

The nubs, the ribs, the stiles.

All that's left.

The refractory rumblestrips
not quite ground all the way down.

And yet,
here is another 'solution',
like some contumaciously overly-familiar
qwerty layout,

altogether
much too ready at hand.